A.I. TO THE RESCUE: HOW ARTIFICIAL INTELLIGENCE CAN HELP HUMANS IN TOUGH SITUATIONS AND MAKE BETTER DECISIONS

BY
HENRY E. PARKINS

COPYRIGHT PAGE

HENRY E. PARKINS

TABLE OF CONTENTS

INTRODUCTION

In an era defined by rapid technological advancements, one innovation stands out as a beacon of hope amidst uncertainty: Artificial Intelligence (A.I.). A.I. to the Rescue: How Artificial Intelligence Can Help Humans in Tough Situations and Make Better Decisions explores the profound impact of A.I. on human endeavors, particularly in navigating challenges and improving decision-making processes.

Artificial Intelligence, once relegated to the realms of science fiction, has now become an integral part of our daily lives. From virtual assistants managing our schedules to sophisticated algorithms powering financial markets, A.I. permeates nearly every aspect of modern society. Yet, its true potential lies beyond mere convenience; it offers a powerful tool for addressing complex problems and enhancing our ability to respond effectively in critical situations.

This book embarks on a journey to uncover the multifaceted ways in which A.I. serves as a force for good, assisting humans in confronting adversity and making more informed choices. Through a comprehensive exploration of various domains, from emergency response and healthcare to finance and environmental conservation, we delve into the transformative capabilities of A.I. and its capacity to augment human capabilities.

The chapters within this book illuminate the remarkable ways in which A.I. contributes to society's resilience and adaptive capacity. We examine how A.I. algorithms predict natural disasters, enable early warning systems, revolutionize medical diagnosis and treatment, optimize financial strategies, preserve our planet's ecosystems, enhance national security measures, and much more. Moreover, we confront the ethical and societal implications inherent in the deployment of A.I., grappling with questions of bias, privacy, and workforce displacement.

As we navigate the complexities of the A.I. landscape, we are reminded of its immense potential to shape the future of humanity. A.I. to the Rescue challenges us to rethink our relationship with technology and embrace the possibilities of collaboration between humans and intelligent machines.

Through thoughtful analysis and compelling narratives, this book offers insights into how we can harness the power of A.I. to confront adversity, make better decisions, and ultimately build a more resilient and prosperous world.

Definition and Brief Overview of Artificial Intelligence (A.I.)

Artificial Intelligence, often abbreviated as A.I., represents the pinnacle of human ingenuity and technological advancement. At its core, A.I. refers to the development of computer systems capable of performing tasks that typically require human intelligence. These tasks encompass a wide spectrum of activities, ranging from problem-solving and decision-making to natural language understanding and pattern recognition.

The concept of Artificial Intelligence traces its roots back to the mid-20th century, when pioneering researchers envisioned machines that could mimic human cognitive functions. Over the decades, A.I. has evolved from theoretical speculation to practical application, fueled by breakthroughs in computer science, mathematics, and neuroscience.

Today, Artificial Intelligence encompasses a diverse array of methodologies and techniques, each tailored to address specific challenges and objectives. Machine learning, a subset of A.I., empowers computers to learn from data without explicit programming, enabling them to identify patterns and make predictions with remarkable accuracy. Deep learning, a subset of machine learning, employs neural networks inspired by the structure and function of the human brain to tackle complex tasks such as image recognition and natural language processing.

The applications of Artificial Intelligence are as vast as they are profound. From virtual assistants like Siri and Alexa to self-driving cars and medical diagnostic systems, A.I. permeates nearly every facet of modern life. In healthcare, A.I. aids in disease diagnosis, drug discovery, and personalized treatment planning. In finance, it powers algorithmic trading strategies, fraud detection systems, and risk management algorithms. In emergency response, A.I. facilitates early warning systems, disaster prediction models, and resource allocation strategies.

Despite its transformative potential, Artificial Intelligence also raises ethical, societal, and philosophical questions that demand careful consideration. Concerns about algorithmic bias, data privacy, and job displacement underscore the need for responsible and inclusive A.I. development practices.

Significance of A.I. in Modern Society

Artificial Intelligence (A.I.) stands as one of the most transformative technologies of the 21st century, wielding profound significance across various facets of modern society. Its impact reverberates through industries, economies, and everyday life, fundamentally altering the way we work, communicate, and interact with the world around us. In the context of "A.I. to the Rescue: How Artificial Intelligence Can Help Humans in Tough Situations and Make Better Decisions," understanding the significance of A.I. illuminates its pivotal role in addressing challenges and improving decision-making processes.

Enhanced Efficiency and Productivity:

A.I. technologies streamline processes, automate routine tasks, and optimize workflows, thereby boosting efficiency and productivity across industries. From manufacturing and logistics to customer service and finance, A.I. systems augment human capabilities, enabling organizations to accomplish more with fewer resources.

Improved Decision Making:

A.I. equips individuals and organizations with data-driven insights and predictive analytics, facilitating informed decision-making in complex and dynamic environments. By analyzing vast datasets and identifying patterns, A.I. algorithms help uncover hidden opportunities, mitigate risks, and guide strategic planning across diverse domains.

Innovation and Creativity:

A.I. fuels innovation by catalyzing the development of novel solutions and groundbreaking technologies. Through machine learning, neural networks, and natural language processing, A.I. empowers researchers, entrepreneurs, and inventors to explore new frontiers, unlock untapped potential, and redefine the boundaries of what is possible.

Personalization and Customization:

A.I. enables hyper-personalized experiences tailored to individual preferences, behaviors, and needs. From personalized recommendations on streaming platforms to adaptive learning algorithms in education, A.I. adapts content and services to suit diverse audiences, fostering deeper engagement and satisfaction.

Advancements in Healthcare:

In healthcare, A.I. revolutionizes patient care, diagnosis, and treatment, driving advancements in precision medicine, medical imaging, and drug discovery. A.I.-powered diagnostic tools enhance accuracy and efficiency, while predictive analytics enable early detection of diseases and proactive interventions, ultimately saving lives and improving health outcomes.

Mitigation of Societal Challenges: A.I. offers innovative solutions to pressing societal challenges, from climate change and environmental conservation to poverty alleviation and disaster response. Through data analysis, modeling, and simulation, A.I. helps policymakers, NGOs, and communities devise effective strategies for sustainable development, resilience-building, and social progress.

Economic Growth and Competitiveness: A.I. catalyzes economic growth by fostering innovation, driving productivity gains, and unlocking new business opportunities. Nations and industries that embrace A.I. technologies gain a competitive edge in the global marketplace, attracting investment, creating jobs, and fueling prosperity.

In sum, the significance of A.I. in modern society extends far beyond technological prowess; it represents a catalyst for positive change, empowerment, and progress.

Purpose of the Book: Exploring How A.I. Aids Humans in Challenging Circumstances and Decision-Making Processes

"A.I. to the Rescue: How Artificial Intelligence Can Help Humans in Tough Situations and Make Better Decisions" is crafted with the aim of delving into the intricate ways in which Artificial Intelligence (A.I.) serves as a crucial asset to humanity, especially during challenging circumstances and in the realm of decision-making processes. The central purpose of this book is to unravel the multifaceted applications of A.I. across diverse scenarios and illuminate its pivotal role in assisting individuals and societies in times of adversity.

In the face of formidable challenges ranging from natural disasters and global pandemics to economic crises and security threats—A.I. emerges as a transformative force, offering innovative solutions and actionable insights that empower humans to navigate complexity and uncertainty with confidence. Through a comprehensive examination of real-world examples, case studies, and expert analyses, this book endeavors to showcase how A.I. enhances decision-making capabilities and augments human resilience in the face of adversity.

By exploring the role of A.I. in emergency response, healthcare delivery, financial management, environmental conservation, and other critical domains, readers will gain profound insights into the ways in which A.I. enables proactive risk mitigation, anticipatory planning, and effective resource allocation. From predictive analytics and early warning systems to personalized recommendations and algorithmic trading strategies, A.I. serves as a catalyst for informed decision-making and strategic foresight.

Moreover, this book seeks to elucidate the ethical, societal, and regulatory considerations inherent in the integration of A.I. into decision-making processes. By addressing issues of transparency, accountability, and algorithmic fairness, readers will be prompted to critically examine the ethical implications of A.I.

adoption and advocate for responsible and equitable deployment of technology.

Ultimately, "A.I. to the Rescue" invites readers on a transformative journey a journey to explore the transformative potential of A.I. as a valuable ally in navigating complexity, overcoming adversity, and making better decisions. Through thoughtful analysis, practical insights, and thought-provoking narratives, this book aims to inspire readers to harness the power of A.I. to tackle tough situations, foster resilience, and forge a path towards a more prosperous and equitable future for all.

CHAPTER 1

UNDERSTANDING ARTIFICIAL INTELLIGENCE

Artificial Intelligence (A.I.) stands at the forefront of technological innovation, representing the culmination of decades of research, experimentation, and advancement in computer science and machine learning. In "A.I. to the Rescue: How Artificial Intelligence Can Help Humans in Tough Situations and Make Better Decisions," it is imperative to develop a comprehensive understanding of A.I. and its underlying principles to appreciate its transformative potential fully.

At its core, Artificial Intelligence refers to the development of computer systems and algorithms capable of performing tasks that traditionally require human intelligence. These tasks encompass a wide range of activities, including problem-solving, decision-making, pattern recognition, language understanding, and learning from experience.

The evolution of Artificial Intelligence can be traced back to the mid-20th century, with the seminal work of pioneers such as Alan Turing, John McCarthy, and Marvin Minsky laying the groundwork for its development. Over time, A.I. has undergone remarkable advancements, driven by breakthroughs in areas such as machine learning, neural networks, natural language processing, and robotics.

Machine learning, a subfield of A.I., forms the bedrock of many contemporary applications, enabling computers to learn from data and improve their performance over time without explicit programming. Supervised learning algorithms learn from labeled datasets, while unsupervised learning algorithms identify patterns and relationships in unlabeled data. Reinforcement learning, inspired by behavioral psychology, involves training algorithms through trial and error to maximize rewards and achieve specific objectives.

Deep learning, a subset of machine learning, employs artificial neural networks inspired by the structure and function of the human brain. These neural networks consist of interconnected layers of artificial neurons that process information and extract features from raw data. Through processes such as convolution, pooling, and backpropagation, deep learning models can achieve unprecedented levels of accuracy and efficiency in tasks such as image recognition, speech recognition, and natural language understanding.

Natural language processing (NLP) enables computers to understand, interpret, and generate human language in a manner that is contextually relevant and semantically meaningful. NLP algorithms analyze text, speech, and other forms of linguistic data to extract insights, summarize information, and facilitate communication between humans and machines.

In "A.I. to the Rescue," it is essential to explore not only the technical underpinnings of Artificial Intelligence but also its practical applications across diverse domains. From healthcare and finance to emergency response and environmental conservation, A.I. is revolutionizing industries, empowering individuals, and reshaping the way we approach complex challenges.

Historical Background of A.I. Development

The historical journey of Artificial Intelligence (A.I.) development is marked by visionary ideas, groundbreaking research, and persistent challenges. In "A.I. to the Rescue: How Artificial Intelligence Can Help Humans in Tough Situations and Make Better Decisions," understanding the historical context of A.I. is essential to appreciate the evolution of this transformative technology.

Origins in Cognitive Science: The roots of A.I. can be traced back to the mid-20th century, with early pioneers such as Alan Turing and John McCarthy laying the groundwork for the field. Turing's seminal work on computability and the Turing Test provided foundational insights into the potential of machines to exhibit intelligent behavior. McCarthy, along with others, coined the term "Artificial Intelligence" and organized the Dartmouth Conference in

1956, which is often regarded as the birth of A.I. as a field of study.

Early Explorations and Symbolic A.I.:

In the 1950s and 1960s, researchers focused on developing symbolic A.I. systems capable of reasoning, problem-solving, and logical inference. Programs like the Logic Theorist and General Problem Solver demonstrated early successes in tackling symbolic reasoning tasks, albeit within limited domains.

The Rise of Machine Learning:

The 1980s witnessed a shift towards machine learning approaches, which emphasized the development of algorithms capable of learning from data and improving performance over time. Researchers explored techniques such as neural networks, genetic algorithms, and expert systems to tackle real-world problems in pattern recognition, language processing, and decision-making.

AI Winter and Resurgence:

The late 1980s and early 1990s saw a period of disillusionment known as the "AI Winter," characterized by waning interest and funding in A.I. research due to overhyped expectations and underwhelming results. However, the field experienced a resurgence in the late 1990s and early 2000s, fueled by advancements in computational power, data availability, and algorithmic sophistication.

Breakthroughs in Deep Learning:
In the 2010s, deep learning emerged as a dominant paradigm within A.I., revolutionizing tasks such as image recognition, speech synthesis, and natural language processing. Deep neural networks, enabled by innovations in model architecture, training algorithms, and hardware acceleration, achieved unprecedented levels of accuracy and performance in complex tasks.

A.I. in the 21st Century: In the 21st century, A.I. has permeated nearly every aspect of modern life, from virtual assistants and autonomous vehicles to medical diagnostics and financial analysis. Rapid advancements in A.I. technologies, coupled with increasing integration into society, have raised new challenges and opportunities related to ethics, fairness, and accountability.

In "A.I. to the Rescue," understanding the historical trajectory of A.I. development provides valuable insights into the challenges, breakthroughs, and paradigm shifts that have shaped the field.

Explanation of Different Types of A.I. Technologies

In "A.I. to the Rescue: How Artificial Intelligence Can Help Humans in Tough Situations and Make Better Decisions," it is essential to understand the diverse array of A.I. technologies that underpin the field's capabilities. These technologies, each with its unique strengths and applications, contribute to the transformative potential of A.I. in addressing challenges and improving decision-making processes.

Machine Learning: Machine learning represents a cornerstone of modern A.I., enabling computers to learn from data and improve performance without explicit programming. Supervised learning algorithms learn from labeled datasets, where inputs are associated with corresponding outputs. Unsupervised learning algorithms identify patterns and relationships in unlabeled data, facilitating tasks such as clustering and anomaly detection. Reinforcement learning involves training algorithms to maximize rewards through trial and error, enabling them to learn optimal strategies in dynamic environments.

Deep Learning: Deep learning is a subset of machine learning that employs artificial neural networks inspired by the structure and function of the human brain. Deep neural networks consist of interconnected layers of artificial neurons, where each layer processes information and extracts features from raw data. Through processes such as convolution, pooling, and backpropagation, deep learning models can achieve remarkable levels of accuracy and efficiency in tasks such as image recognition, speech synthesis, and natural language processing.

Natural Language Processing (NLP): Natural language processing enables computers to understand, interpret, and generate human language in a manner that is contextually relevant and semantically meaningful. NLP algorithms analyze text, speech, and other forms of linguistic data to extract insights, summarize information, and facilitate communication between humans and machines. Applications of NLP include language translation, sentiment analysis, text summarization, and conversational agents.

Computer Vision: Computer vision is a branch of A.I. that focuses on enabling computers to interpret and analyze visual information from the real world. Computer vision algorithms process images and videos to extract features, detect objects, recognize patterns, and infer spatial relationships. Applications of computer vision include object detection, facial recognition, autonomous driving, medical imaging, and surveillance systems.

Robotics: Robotics integrates A.I. technologies with physical systems to create autonomous machines capable of sensing, reasoning, and acting in the real world. Robotics encompasses a wide range of applications, including industrial automation, healthcare robotics, service robots, and autonomous drones. A.I. plays a crucial role in enabling robots to perceive their environment, make decisions, and adapt to changing circumstances.

Explanation of Different Types of A.I. Technologies

In "A.I. to the Rescue: How Artificial Intelligence Can Help Humans in Tough Situations and Make Better Decisions," it's crucial to understand the diverse array of A.I. technologies that contribute to enhancing human capabilities and decision-making processes. Here's an explanation of some key types of A.I. technologies:

Machine Learning (ML): Machine learning is a subset of artificial intelligence that enables systems to learn from data and improve performance over time without being explicitly programmed. ML algorithms can be categorized into three main types:

Supervised Learning: In supervised learning, algorithms learn from labeled data, making predictions or decisions based on input-output pairs.

Unsupervised Learning:

Unsupervised learning algorithms learn patterns and relationships from unlabeled data, identifying inherent structures or clusters within the data.

Reinforcement Learning:

Reinforcement learning involves training algorithms to make sequences of decisions by rewarding desired behaviors and penalizing undesired ones.

Neural Networks:

Neural networks are computational models inspired by the structure and function of the human brain. They consist of interconnected nodes, or neurons, organized into layers. Different types of neural networks include:

Feedforward Neural Networks:

In feedforward neural networks, information flows in one direction from input to output—without feedback loops.

Recurrent Neural Networks (RNNs):

RNNs are designed to process sequences of data, making them well-suited for tasks such as natural language processing and time-series analysis.

Convolutional Neural Networks (CNNs): CNNs are specialized neural networks for processing grid-like data, such as images. They utilize convolutional layers to extract features hierarchically.

Natural Language Processing (NLP): Natural language processing is a branch of artificial intelligence focused on enabling computers to understand, interpret, and generate human language. NLP encompasses various tasks, including:

Text Classification: Classifying text documents into predefined categories or labels.

Named Entity Recognition (NER): Identifying and classifying named entities (e.g., names of people, organizations, locations) within text.

Sentiment Analysis: Determining the sentiment or emotional tone of text, such as positive, negative, or neutral.

Language Translation: Translating text from one language to another using machine translation algorithms.

Expert Systems: Expert systems are A.I. programs designed to emulate the decision-making abilities of human experts in specific domains. They rely on knowledge bases, inference engines, and rule-based reasoning to provide recommendations or solutions to complex problems.

Reinforcement Learning: Reinforcement learning is a type of machine learning where an agent learns to make decisions by interacting with an environment and receiving feedback in the form of rewards or penalties. It is often used in scenarios where the optimal action depends on the current state of the environment.

Examples of A.I. Applications in Various Fields

Healthcare:
Medical Diagnosis: A.I.-powered diagnostic systems, such as IBM Watson for Oncology, assist healthcare professionals in accurately diagnosing diseases and recommending treatment plans based on patient data and medical literature.

Drug Discovery: A.I. algorithms analyze molecular structures, biological data, and clinical trial results to accelerate the discovery and development of new drugs and therapies, reducing the time and cost associated with traditional drug discovery processes.

Emergency Response:

Disaster Prediction and Management: A.I. models analyze historical data, weather patterns, and geographical information to predict natural disasters such as earthquakes, hurricanes, and wildfires, enabling authorities to evacuate populations and allocate resources more effectively.

Early Warning Systems: A.I.-driven early warning systems monitor various parameters, such as seismic activity and weather patterns, to provide timely alerts and warnings to communities at risk of natural disasters or emergencies.

Finance:

Algorithmic Trading: A.I.-powered trading algorithms analyze market trends, news articles, and social media sentiment to execute high-frequency trades and optimize investment strategies, resulting in improved returns and reduced trading risks.

Fraud Detection: A.I. algorithms analyze transaction data, user behavior, and historical patterns to detect and prevent fraudulent activities in banking, credit card transactions, and online payments.

Environmental Conservation:

Wildlife Monitoring: A.I.-enabled camera traps and sensors analyze images and audio recordings to identify and track endangered species, monitor habitat loss, and detect illegal poaching activities in conservation areas.

Climate Modeling: A.I.-driven climate models analyze vast amounts of atmospheric and oceanic data to predict climate change trends, assess the impact of human activities on the environment, and inform policy decisions aimed at mitigating climate-related risks.

Education:

Personalized Learning: A.I.-powered adaptive learning platforms analyze students' learning styles, performance data, and preferences to deliver personalized learning experiences tailored to individual needs and abilities, improving student engagement and academic outcomes.

Intelligent Tutoring Systems: A.I.-based tutoring systems provide students with interactive learning experiences, adaptive feedback, and personalized recommendations to enhance comprehension and mastery of academic subjects.

Transportation:

Autonomous Vehicles: A.I.-driven autonomous vehicles use sensors, cameras, and machine learning algorithms to navigate roads, detect obstacles, and make real-time driving decisions, reducing accidents and improving traffic flow.

Traffic Management: A.I.-powered traffic management systems analyze traffic patterns, congestion data, and real-time GPS information to optimize traffic signals, reroute vehicles, and reduce commute times in urban areas.

CHAPTER 2

THE ROLE OF A.I. IN DISASTER PREDICTION AND PREVENTION

In the face of natural disasters and emergencies, Artificial Intelligence (A.I.) emerges as a pivotal tool in predicting, mitigating, and preventing catastrophic events. This chapter delves into the transformative role of A.I. in disaster prediction and prevention, highlighting its applications, benefits, and potential to save lives and protect communities.

Early Warning Systems:

A.I.-powered early warning systems analyze vast amounts of data, including meteorological data, seismic activity, and environmental indicators, to detect potential hazards such as earthquakes, tsunamis, hurricanes, and wildfires.

By leveraging machine learning algorithms and predictive analytics, A.I. models can forecast the likelihood, intensity, and trajectory of natural disasters with greater accuracy and precision.

Early warning systems issue timely alerts to at-risk populations, enabling authorities to implement preventive measures, evacuate affected areas, and mobilize resources proactively, thereby saving lives and reducing the impact of disasters.

Predictive Analytics:

A.I. algorithms analyze historical data and patterns to predict future trends and identify high-risk areas prone to natural disasters.

By integrating satellite imagery, climate models, and geospatial data, A.I. models can identify vulnerable regions and assess the potential impact of environmental factors such as deforestation, urbanization, and climate change on disaster occurrence and severity.

Risk Assessment and Vulnerability Mapping:

A.I.-driven risk assessment tools evaluate the vulnerability of infrastructure, communities, and ecosystems to natural disasters.

A.I. algorithms analyze socio-economic factors, population density, and land-use patterns to identify areas at greater risk of flooding, landslides, or other catastrophic events.

Vulnerability mapping enables policymakers, urban planners, and emergency responders to prioritize resources, implement mitigation strategies, and develop resilient infrastructure to withstand the impact of disasters.

Early Detection of Environmental Changes:

A.I. technologies, such as remote sensing and satellite monitoring, enable real-time detection of environmental changes and anomalies.

A.I. algorithms analyze sensor data, imagery, and atmospheric conditions to detect early warning signs of potential disasters, such as abnormal weather patterns, rising sea levels, or seismic activity.

Early detection allows for timely intervention, risk mitigation measures, and community preparedness efforts to minimize the impact of environmental hazards.

Adaptive Response and Decision Support:

A.I.-powered decision support systems assist emergency responders, government agencies, and humanitarian organizations in developing adaptive response strategies and allocating resources effectively during disasters.

A.I. models analyze real-time data feeds, social media trends, and crowd-sourced information to generate actionable insights and situational awareness for decision-makers.

Adaptive response strategies enable authorities to coordinate rescue operations, deploy emergency services, and provide aid to affected populations in a timely and efficient manner.

Utilization of A.I. for Early Warning Systems

In the face of natural disasters and emergencies, early warning systems play a crucial role in saving lives, minimizing damage, and facilitating timely response efforts. This chapter explores how Artificial Intelligence (A.I.) is revolutionizing early warning systems, enhancing their accuracy, effectiveness, and responsiveness to emerging threats.

Data Integration and Analysis:

A.I.-powered early warning systems integrate diverse sources of data, including meteorological data, seismic activity, satellite imagery, and social media feeds.

Machine learning algorithms analyze large volumes of real-time data to detect patterns, trends, and anomalies indicative of potential hazards, such as earthquakes, tsunamis, hurricanes, and wildfires.

Predictive Modeling:

A.I. models utilize historical data and predictive analytics to forecast the likelihood, intensity, and trajectory of natural disasters.

By analyzing past events, environmental conditions, and climate patterns, A.I. algorithms can predict the probability of future disasters and issue timely warnings to at-risk populations.

Real-Time Monitoring and Alerting:

A.I.-driven early warning systems monitor environmental conditions, sensor readings, and atmospheric changes in real-time.

Through continuous data analysis and anomaly detection, A.I. algorithms can identify sudden shifts or deviations from normal patterns, triggering immediate alerts and notifications to authorities and the public.

Localized Risk Assessment:

A.I. technologies enable localized risk assessment and vulnerability mapping, taking into account factors such as population density, infrastructure resilience, and socio-economic disparities.

By analyzing spatial data and demographic information, A.I. models can identify high-risk areas and prioritize early warning efforts in communities most susceptible to natural disasters.

Adaptive Response Strategies:

A.I.-powered early warning systems support the development of adaptive response strategies tailored to specific disaster scenarios.

By considering factors such as population demographics, evacuation routes, and emergency resources, A.I. algorithms assist authorities in formulating contingency plans and allocating resources effectively in anticipation of disaster events.

Community Engagement and Communication:

A.I.-driven early warning systems facilitate community engagement and public awareness through targeted communication and outreach efforts.

Interactive platforms, chatbots, and mobile applications powered by A.I. technologies deliver personalized alerts, safety tips, and evacuation instructions to individuals and households, fostering a culture of preparedness and resilience.

Case Studies of A.I. Implementation in Emergency Situations

Hurricane Tracking and Prediction:

During the Atlantic hurricane season, A.I. plays a crucial role in tracking and predicting the path and intensity of storms. Organizations like the National Hurricane Center leverage A.I. algorithms to analyze satellite imagery, weather data, and historical patterns to forecast hurricane trajectories and issue timely warnings to coastal communities. A.I. models such as neural networks and ensemble methods improve the accuracy of hurricane forecasting, enabling authorities to implement evacuation plans, mobilize emergency responders, and mitigate the impact of hurricanes on lives and infrastructure.

Earthquake Early Warning Systems:

In earthquake-prone regions like Japan and California, A.I.-powered early warning systems provide vital seconds of advance notice to residents and businesses before the onset of seismic waves. The Japan Meteorological Agency's Earthquake Early Warning system employs A.I. algorithms to detect initial tremors, estimate earthquake magnitudes, and disseminate alerts through television, radio, and mobile devices. By integrating real-time seismic data and predictive models, A.I. enables individuals to take immediate actions to seek shelter, stop machinery, and prevent injuries during earthquakes.

Pandemic Surveillance and Monitoring:

During the COVID-19 pandemic, A.I. technologies have been instrumental in tracking the spread of the virus, identifying hotspots, and informing public health interventions. The use of A.I.-powered predictive models and data analytics platforms enables health authorities to analyze epidemiological trends, hospitalization rates, and vaccination coverage in real-time. Companies like BlueDot employ A.I. algorithms to analyze global news reports, flight itineraries, and social media data to detect outbreaks and assess pandemic risk levels, facilitating early response efforts and resource allocation in affected regions.

Wildfire Detection and Management:

In regions prone to wildfires, A.I. plays a critical role in early detection and response to forest fires. Systems like the FireSat constellation utilize A.I.-enabled satellite imagery and infrared sensors to monitor vegetation health, detect heat signatures, and identify potential fire outbreaks in remote areas. A.I. algorithms analyze historical fire data, weather patterns, and terrain characteristics to predict fire behavior, assess fire risk levels, and prioritize firefighting efforts. By providing early warnings and situational awareness to firefighters and emergency responders, A.I. helps minimize property damage, protect ecosystems, and save lives during wildfire incidents.

Flood Prediction and Disaster Management:

In flood-prone regions, A.I.-driven flood prediction models enable authorities to anticipate rising water levels, assess flood risks, and implement preventive measures to safeguard communities and infrastructure. Projects like Flood AI leverage machine learning algorithms to analyze hydrological data, rainfall patterns, and topographic maps to predict flood events and generate inundation maps. By simulating flood scenarios and evaluating mitigation strategies, A.I. supports urban planners, emergency managers, and policymakers in enhancing flood resilience, improving drainage systems, and reducing the impact of flooding on vulnerable populations.

CHAPTER 3

A.I. IN HEALTHCARE DECISION MAKING

In the ever-evolving landscape of healthcare, Artificial Intelligence (A.I.) emerges as a powerful tool in aiding clinical decision-making, improving patient outcomes, and optimizing healthcare delivery. This chapter explores the transformative role of A.I. in healthcare decision-making processes, highlighting its applications, benefits, and potential to revolutionize patient care.

Medical Imaging and Diagnosis:

A.I. algorithms analyze medical imaging data, including X-rays, MRIs, and CT scans, to assist radiologists and clinicians in detecting abnormalities, identifying diseases, and making accurate diagnoses.

Deep learning models, such as convolutional neural networks (CNNs), enhance image interpretation by highlighting suspicious regions, quantifying lesion characteristics, and providing diagnostic insights with high accuracy and efficiency.

Clinical Decision Support Systems (CDSS):

A.I.-powered clinical decision support systems integrate patient data, electronic health records (EHRs), and medical literature to provide evidence-based recommendations and treatment guidelines to healthcare providers.

CDSS algorithms assist physicians in diagnosing diseases, selecting appropriate treatment options, and predicting patient outcomes based on clinical data, historical trends, and best practices.

Personalized Medicine and Treatment Planning:

A.I. enables personalized medicine by analyzing genomic data, molecular profiles, and patient demographics to tailor treatment plans and interventions based on individual characteristics and genetic predispositions.

Machine learning algorithms identify biomarkers, predict drug responses, and optimize treatment regimens to improve therapeutic efficacy, minimize adverse effects, and enhance patient satisfaction.

Predictive Analytics and Risk Stratification:

A.I. models leverage predictive analytics to forecast patient outcomes, anticipate disease progression, and stratify individuals based on their risk profiles.

By analyzing longitudinal data, vital signs, and comorbidity patterns, predictive algorithms identify patients at high risk of complications, hospital readmissions, or adverse events, enabling early intervention and preventive care strategies.

Drug Discovery and Development:

A.I. accelerates drug discovery and development by simulating molecular interactions, predicting drug-target interactions, and screening compound libraries for therapeutic candidates.

Machine learning algorithms facilitate virtual screening, de novo drug design, and structure-activity relationship modeling, leading to the identification of novel drug candidates and the repurposing of existing medications for new indications.

Healthcare Resource Allocation and Optimization:

A.I. algorithms optimize healthcare resource allocation by forecasting patient demand, predicting hospital admissions, and scheduling medical procedures to maximize efficiency and minimize wait times.

By analyzing operational data, patient flow patterns, and staffing requirements, A.I.-driven optimization tools help healthcare organizations improve resource utilization, streamline workflows, and enhance patient access to timely and quality care.

As "A.I. to the Rescue" illuminates, leveraging Artificial Intelligence in healthcare decision-making empowers clinicians, researchers, and policymakers to make informed decisions, improve patient outcomes, and enhance the overall quality and efficiency of healthcare delivery. However, it also underscores the importance of ethical considerations, regulatory compliance, and human oversight in integrating A.I. technologies into clinical practice.

Diagnosis and Treatment Planning Using A.I.

In the realm of healthcare, the integration of Artificial Intelligence (A.I.) presents transformative opportunities in diagnosis and treatment planning, revolutionizing the way medical conditions are identified, assessed, and managed. This chapter delves into the remarkable advancements made possible by A.I. in healthcare decision-making processes, highlighting its role in diagnosis and personalized treatment planning.

Medical Imaging Interpretation:

A.I. algorithms analyze medical images such as X-rays, CT scans, and MRIs to assist radiologists and clinicians in detecting anomalies and diagnosing conditions.

Convolutional Neural Networks (CNNs) and deep learning models can identify patterns, lesions, and abnormalities with high accuracy, enabling early detection of diseases such as cancer, cardiovascular conditions, and neurological disorders.

Pathology and Histopathology Analysis:

A.I. tools aid pathologists in analyzing tissue samples and identifying cellular abnormalities indicative of diseases such as cancer, infections, and autoimmune disorders.

Machine learning algorithms analyze histopathological images to classify cell types, grade tumors, and predict disease prognosis, facilitating accurate diagnosis and treatment planning.

Clinical Decision Support Systems (CDSS):

A.I.-powered CDSS platforms integrate patient data, electronic health records (EHRs), and clinical guidelines to provide evidence-based recommendations to healthcare providers.

CDSS algorithms assist clinicians in diagnosing conditions, selecting appropriate treatment options, and predicting patient outcomes based on individual health profiles and medical history.

Genomic Analysis and Personalized Medicine:

A.I. enables personalized medicine by analyzing genomic data, gene expression profiles, and molecular biomarkers to tailor treatment plans and therapies to individual patients.

Machine learning algorithms identify genetic mutations, predict drug responses, and recommend targeted therapies, improving treatment efficacy and minimizing adverse effects.

Disease Risk Assessment and Stratification:

A.I. models leverage predictive analytics to assess disease risk, predict patient outcomes, and stratify individuals based on their health status and susceptibility to specific conditions.

By analyzing patient demographics, clinical data, and lifestyle factors, predictive algorithms identify individuals at high risk of developing diseases such as diabetes, heart disease, and cancer, enabling early intervention and preventive care strategies.

Treatment Optimization and Drug Discovery:

A.I. accelerates treatment optimization and drug discovery by simulating molecular interactions, predicting drug-target interactions, and screening compound libraries for potential therapeutic candidates.

Machine learning algorithms facilitate virtual screening, de novo drug design, and structure-activity relationship modeling, leading to the discovery of novel drug candidates and the repurposing of existing medications for new indications.

Personalized Medicine and A.I.-Driven Therapies

Personalized medicine, empowered by Artificial Intelligence (A.I.), represents a groundbreaking approach to healthcare delivery, offering tailored treatments and interventions based on individual patient characteristics and genetic profiles. This chapter explores the transformative potential of personalized medicine and A.I.-driven therapies in revolutionizing patient care and improving health outcomes.

Genomic Analysis and Precision Medicine:

A.I. algorithms analyze genomic data, gene expression patterns, and molecular biomarkers to identify genetic predispositions, disease susceptibilities, and therapeutic targets.

By sequencing individual genomes and decoding genetic variations, personalized medicine enables clinicians to customize treatment plans, predict drug responses, and optimize therapeutic interventions for each patient.

Drug Response Prediction and Optimization:

A.I. facilitates drug response prediction by modeling drug-target interactions, pharmacokinetics, and patient-specific factors to anticipate individual responses to medications.

Machine learning algorithms analyze patient data, clinical records, and genetic profiles to identify biomarkers, predict adverse reactions, and recommend optimal drug dosages, enhancing treatment efficacy and minimizing adverse effects.

Targeted Therapies and Immunotherapy:

A.I.-driven targeted therapies exploit molecular targets and pathways implicated in disease progression, enabling precise interventions tailored to the unique biology of each patient.

Immunotherapy harnesses the body's immune system to target and eradicate cancer cells, with A.I. algorithms guiding the selection of immunotherapeutic agents, predicting treatment response, and monitoring immune-related adverse events.

Predictive Modeling and Treatment Outcomes:

A.I. models leverage predictive analytics to forecast treatment outcomes, anticipate disease progression, and stratify patients based on their risk profiles.

By analyzing patient data, clinical parameters, and treatment histories, predictive algorithms inform clinicians about prognosis, guide treatment decisions, and facilitate shared decision-making between patients and healthcare providers.

Real-Time Monitoring and Adaptive Therapies:

A.I.-powered monitoring systems track patient health metrics, biomarkers, and physiological parameters in real-time, enabling early detection of treatment responses and disease progression.

Continuous monitoring facilitates adaptive therapies, where treatment regimens are dynamically adjusted based on patient feedback, treatment efficacy, and evolving disease status, optimizing therapeutic outcomes and minimizing treatment-related complications.

Clinical Trials and Drug Development:

A.I. accelerates drug discovery and development by predicting drug candidates, optimizing lead compounds, and identifying patient subpopulations likely to benefit from novel therapies.

Machine learning algorithms analyze large-scale biomedical data, chemical structures, and drug-target interactions to expedite preclinical testing, prioritize drug candidates for clinical trials, and streamline the drug development pipeline.

Ethical Considerations and Challenges in Healthcare A.I.

As Artificial Intelligence (A.I.) continues to permeate healthcare, it brings forth a myriad of ethical considerations and challenges that demand careful attention and thoughtful deliberation. This chapter delves into the ethical implications of integrating A.I. in healthcare and explores the challenges faced by stakeholders in navigating the complexities of A.I.-driven medical interventions.

Data Privacy and Security:

A.I. systems rely on vast amounts of sensitive patient data, including medical records, genomic information, and diagnostic imaging. Ensuring the privacy and security of patient data is paramount to maintaining patient trust and confidentiality.

Ethical considerations include implementing robust data encryption measures, obtaining informed consent for data usage, and adhering to regulatory frameworks such as the Health Insurance Portability and Accountability Act (HIPAA) to safeguard patient privacy.

Bias and Fairness in Algorithms:

A.I. algorithms may inadvertently perpetuate biases present in the data used for training, leading to disparities in healthcare delivery and outcomes across different demographic groups.

Ethical challenges include identifying and mitigating algorithmic bias, ensuring fairness and equity in healthcare decision-making, and promoting transparency and accountability in algorithm development and deployment.

Clinical Interpretability and Transparency:

A.I. models often operate as "black boxes," making it challenging for healthcare providers to understand the rationale behind their recommendations and decisions.

Ethical considerations include promoting model interpretability and transparency, providing clinicians with insights into A.I. predictions and underlying decision processes, and fostering trust and collaboration between humans and machines in clinical practice.

Patient Autonomy and Informed Consent:

A.I.-driven healthcare interventions may impact patient autonomy and decision-making, raising questions about the extent to which patients should be involved in A.I.-assisted treatment decisions.

Ethical challenges include ensuring informed consent for A.I.-enabled medical procedures, educating patients about the benefits and risks of A.I. interventions, and respecting patient preferences and values in the healthcare decision-making process.

Professional Responsibility and Liability:

A.I. systems augment, but do not replace, the expertise of healthcare professionals, raising questions about professional responsibility, liability, and accountability in the event of errors or adverse outcomes.

Ethical considerations include defining the roles and responsibilities of healthcare providers and A.I. systems, establishing clear lines of communication and collaboration between humans and machines, and developing mechanisms for addressing legal and ethical implications of A.I.-driven medical interventions.

Equitable Access and Healthcare Disparities:

A.I. has the potential to exacerbate existing healthcare disparities if access to A.I.-enabled healthcare interventions is unequal or if vulnerable populations are disproportionately impacted by algorithmic biases.

Ethical challenges include ensuring equitable access to A.I.-driven healthcare technologies, addressing digital divides and disparities in healthcare access, and promoting inclusivity and diversity in A.I. research and development efforts.

CHAPTER 4

CHAPTER: A.I. IN FINANCIAL DECISION MAKING

In the realm of finance, Artificial Intelligence (A.I.) is revolutionizing the way financial decisions are made, offering powerful tools and predictive models to enhance investment strategies, manage risks, and optimize portfolio performance. This chapter explores the transformative role of A.I. in financial decision-making processes, highlighting its applications, benefits, and potential to reshape the financial landscape.

Algorithmic Trading and Quantitative Analysis:

A.I. algorithms analyze vast amounts of financial data, market trends, and historical patterns to identify trading opportunities, execute trades, and optimize investment strategies.

Machine learning models, such as neural networks and reinforcement learning

59

algorithms, enable high-frequency trading firms and hedge funds to make split-second decisions, exploit market inefficiencies, and generate alpha in volatile market conditions.

Predictive Analytics and Market Forecasting:

A.I. models leverage predictive analytics to forecast market trends, predict asset price movements, and anticipate changes in investor sentiment.

By analyzing macroeconomic indicators, sentiment analysis, and alternative data sources, A.I.-driven forecasting tools assist traders and investors in making informed decisions, managing risks, and capitalizing on emerging opportunities in financial markets.

Portfolio Optimization and Asset Allocation:

A.I.-powered portfolio optimization tools utilize advanced optimization algorithms to construct diversified portfolios, allocate assets, and rebalance investment holdings based on risk preferences and investment objectives.

Machine learning algorithms analyze historical returns, covariance matrices, and correlation structures to optimize portfolio weights, minimize volatility, and enhance risk-adjusted returns for investors.

Risk Management and Fraud Detection:

A.I. algorithms employ advanced risk models and anomaly detection techniques to identify fraudulent activities, detect suspicious transactions, and mitigate operational risks in financial institutions.

By analyzing transactional data, user behavior patterns, and network activities, A.I.-driven fraud detection systems help banks, payment processors, and fintech companies combat financial crimes and safeguard against cyber threats.

Credit Scoring and Loan Underwriting:

A.I. models automate credit scoring and loan underwriting processes by analyzing borrower profiles, credit histories, and financial indicators to assess creditworthiness and determine loan eligibility.

Machine learning algorithms predict default probabilities, estimate loss given default (LGD), and calculate expected credit losses (ECL), enabling lenders to make data-driven lending decisions, streamline loan origination workflows, and improve credit risk management practices.

Customer Relationship Management (CRM) and Personalized Finance:

A.I.-powered CRM systems leverage customer data, transaction histories, and behavioral insights to deliver personalized financial recommendations, tailored product offerings, and targeted marketing campaigns.

By analyzing customer preferences, spending patterns, and life events, A.I. algorithms enable financial institutions to deepen customer relationships, enhance customer engagement, and drive business growth through targeted cross-selling and upselling initiatives.

Algorithmic Trading and Risk Management

In the dynamic and fast-paced world of financial markets, Algorithmic Trading and Risk Management have emerged as critical components of investment strategies, leveraging Artificial Intelligence (A.I.) to navigate volatility, capitalize on opportunities, and mitigate risks. This chapter explores the transformative role of A.I. in algorithmic trading and risk management, highlighting its applications, benefits, and potential to enhance financial decision-making.

Algorithmic Trading Strategies:

A.I. algorithms analyze vast amounts of financial data, market indicators, and trading signals to execute buy and sell orders at optimal prices and timings.

Machine learning models, such as neural networks and reinforcement learning algorithms, identify patterns, exploit market inefficiencies, and execute trades with speed and precision, enabling traders to capitalize on short-term price movements and market fluctuations.

63

High-Frequency Trading (HFT):

A.I.-powered high-frequency trading strategies leverage advanced algorithms and low-latency infrastructure to execute large volumes of trades within milliseconds.

By exploiting microstructural patterns, order flow dynamics, and market liquidity, high-frequency traders profit from small price discrepancies and arbitrage opportunities, contributing to market liquidity and price efficiency.

Market Microstructure Analysis:

A.I. models analyze market microstructure data, order book dynamics, and trade execution patterns to understand market liquidity, price impact, and order flow dynamics.

Machine learning algorithms identify trading signals, predict market trends, and optimize execution strategies, enabling traders to minimize transaction costs, reduce slippage, and improve trade execution quality.

Risk Management and Portfolio Optimization:

A.I. algorithms employ sophisticated risk models and portfolio optimization techniques to manage portfolio volatility, mitigate downside risk, and optimize risk-adjusted returns.

By analyzing portfolio characteristics, asset correlations, and market risk factors, risk management systems provide investors with insights into portfolio risk exposures, stress testing scenarios, and potential drawdowns.

Market Surveillance and Compliance:

A.I.-driven surveillance systems monitor trading activities, detect market abuses, and ensure compliance with regulatory requirements and industry standards.

Machine learning algorithms analyze transactional data, order flows, and trade patterns to identify suspicious activities, detect market manipulation, and enforce market integrity rules.

Quantitative Risk Analysis and Stress Testing:

A.I. models enable quantitative risk analysis and stress testing of investment portfolios, financial instruments, and trading strategies.

By simulating market scenarios, assessing tail risks, and quantifying potential losses, risk management frameworks help investors understand the impact of adverse market events and implement risk mitigation strategies.

Fraud Detection and Prevention Using A.I.

In the realm of finance and cybersecurity, Fraud Detection and Prevention stand as critical pillars safeguarding against financial crimes and security breaches. Leveraging the capabilities of Artificial Intelligence (A.I.), organizations can fortify their defenses, detect fraudulent activities, and mitigate risks effectively. This chapter explores the pivotal role of A.I. in fraud detection and prevention, illustrating its applications, benefits, and potential to combat fraud in various sectors.

Anomaly Detection and Pattern Recognition:

A.I. algorithms analyze vast volumes of transactional data, user behaviors, and network activities to detect anomalies and identify suspicious patterns indicative of fraudulent activities.

Machine learning models, such as unsupervised learning and clustering algorithms, flag unusual behaviors, outlier transactions, and deviations from normal patterns, enabling early detection and intervention.

Behavioral Analysis and User Profiling:

A.I.-driven behavioral analysis techniques profile user behaviors, transaction histories, and digital footprints to identify fraudulent activities and assess risk levels.

By monitoring user interactions, navigation paths, and transactional patterns, A.I. algorithms establish baseline behaviors, detect deviations, and recognize fraudulent patterns in real-time.

Predictive Analytics and Risk Scoring:

A.I. models leverage predictive analytics to assess fraud risk scores, predict fraudulent transactions, and prioritize alerts for investigation.

By analyzing historical data, fraud patterns, and risk indicators, predictive algorithms identify high-risk transactions, fraudulent accounts, and suspicious activities, enabling proactive risk management and fraud prevention measures.

Natural Language Processing (NLP) and Text Mining:

A.I. techniques such as Natural Language Processing (NLP) and text mining analyze unstructured data, textual descriptions, and communications to uncover fraudulent schemes and illicit activities.

NLP algorithms parse text documents, chat logs, and email communications to detect fraudulent content, phishing attempts, and social engineering tactics, enabling organizations to identify and mitigate emerging threats.

Network Analysis and Link Prediction:

A.I.-powered network analysis tools examine relationships, connections, and associations between entities to uncover fraud rings, money laundering schemes, and organized criminal activities.

By analyzing transaction networks, social graphs, and communication patterns, network analysis algorithms identify suspicious links, detect collusion among fraudsters, and disrupt illicit networks.

Continuous Monitoring and Adaptive Learning:

A.I.-driven fraud detection systems provide continuous monitoring and adaptive learning capabilities to adapt to evolving fraud patterns and emerging threats.

By leveraging real-time data feeds, dynamic models, and feedback loops, A.I. algorithms update fraud detection rules, refine risk models, and enhance detection accuracy, ensuring proactive detection and prevention of fraudulent activities.

A.I.-Powered Financial Advising and Investment Strategies

In the ever-evolving landscape of finance, Artificial Intelligence (A.I.) is revolutionizing the way individuals manage their wealth, make investment decisions, and plan for their financial future. This chapter delves into the transformative role of A.I. in financial advising and investment strategies, showcasing its applications, benefits, and potential to empower investors and optimize portfolio performance.

Robo-Advisors and Automated Investment Platforms:

A.I.-powered robo-advisors leverage algorithms and machine learning models to provide personalized investment advice, asset allocation strategies, and portfolio management solutions.

By analyzing investor preferences, risk tolerance levels, and financial goals, robo-advisors recommend diversified portfolios, rebalance asset allocations, and optimize investment strategies in a cost-effective and efficient manner.

Predictive Analytics and Market Forecasting:

A.I. models utilize predictive analytics to forecast market trends, predict asset price movements, and identify investment opportunities across diverse asset classes.

Machine learning algorithms analyze historical data, market indicators, and economic factors to generate investment signals, timing entry and exit points, and maximizing returns while minimizing risks.

Quantitative Trading Strategies and Algorithmic Trading:

A.I.-driven quantitative trading strategies employ advanced algorithms and quantitative models to execute trades, manage risk, and capitalize on market inefficiencies.

By leveraging statistical arbitrage, trend-following strategies, and mean reversion techniques, algorithmic trading systems generate alpha and enhance portfolio performance in dynamic and volatile market conditions.

Sentiment Analysis and Social Media Monitoring:

A.I. techniques such as sentiment analysis and social media monitoring analyze news sentiment, market sentiment, and social media chatter to gauge investor sentiment and market sentiment.

By monitoring online conversations, news headlines, and social media trends, A.I. algorithms identify market sentiment shifts, detect market rumors, and anticipate investor behavior, enabling informed decision-making and proactive risk management.

Portfolio Optimization and Risk Management:

A.I.-powered portfolio optimization tools employ sophisticated risk models and optimization algorithms to construct diversified portfolios, manage risk exposures, and enhance risk-adjusted returns.

Machine learning algorithms analyze asset correlations, covariance matrices, and risk factors to optimize portfolio weights, minimize volatility, and achieve desired risk-return profiles for investors.

72

Personalized Finance and Behavioral Economics:

A.I.-driven personalized finance solutions integrate behavioral economics principles and psychological insights to understand investor behavior, biases, and decision-making processes.

By tailoring investment recommendations, nudging behavioral changes, and providing personalized feedback, A.I. systems empower investors to make informed decisions, overcome cognitive biases, and achieve financial goals.

CHAPTER 5

CHAPTER: A.I. IN ENVIRONMENTAL CONSERVATION

In the face of escalating environmental challenges and biodiversity loss, Artificial Intelligence (A.I.) emerges as a powerful ally in the quest for environmental conservation and sustainability. This chapter explores the multifaceted applications of A.I. in environmental conservation efforts, highlighting its role in monitoring ecosystems, protecting endangered species, and mitigating the impacts of climate change.

Biodiversity Monitoring and Species Identification:

A.I. algorithms analyze remote sensing data, satellite imagery, and ecological datasets to monitor biodiversity hotspots, track species populations, and assess habitat health.

Machine learning models employ image recognition and classification techniques to identify species, detect wildlife habitats, and map ecological communities, enabling conservationists to prioritize conservation efforts and implement targeted interventions.

Illegal Wildlife Trafficking Detection:

A.I.-powered systems leverage image analysis, natural language processing, and data mining to identify patterns of illegal wildlife trafficking, poaching activities, and trade routes.

By analyzing online marketplaces, social media platforms, and transportation networks, A.I. algorithms detect illicit wildlife products, disrupt criminal networks, and facilitate law enforcement efforts to combat wildlife crime.

Habitat Restoration and Land Management:

A.I. models optimize land management practices, reforestation efforts, and habitat restoration projects by analyzing ecological data, soil compositions, and climate patterns.

Machine learning algorithms recommend optimal planting strategies, prioritize restoration sites, and predict ecosystem responses to environmental changes, enhancing the resilience and functionality of natural habitats.

Climate Change Modeling and Prediction:

A.I.-driven climate models simulate climate dynamics, predict weather patterns, and assess the impacts of climate change on ecosystems, biodiversity, and human communities.

By integrating meteorological data, climate projections, and environmental variables, A.I. algorithms forecast extreme weather events, identify vulnerable regions, and inform adaptation strategies to mitigate the risks of climate-related disasters.

Precision Conservation and Resource Management:

A.I.-powered precision conservation tools optimize resource allocation, land use planning, and conservation interventions by analyzing spatial data, ecosystem services, and socio-economic factors.

Machine learning algorithms identify conservation priorities, optimize protected area design, and quantify ecosystem services value, facilitating evidence-based decision-making and maximizing conservation outcomes.

Citizen Science and Community Engagement:

A.I.-enabled citizen science platforms engage volunteers, communities, and stakeholders in environmental monitoring, data collection, and conservation initiatives.

By crowdsourcing biodiversity observations, collecting environmental data, and fostering public participation, A.I. platforms empower citizens to contribute to conservation efforts, raise awareness, and advocate for environmental stewardship.

Monitoring and Managing Natural Resources with A.I.

In the era of rapid environmental degradation and resource depletion, the application of Artificial Intelligence (A.I.) holds immense promise for monitoring and

77

managing natural resources sustainably. This chapter explores the innovative ways in which A.I. is revolutionizing resource management practices, enhancing conservation efforts, and promoting environmental sustainability across diverse ecosystems.

Remote Sensing and Geospatial Analysis:

A.I. algorithms process satellite imagery, aerial surveys, and geospatial data to monitor changes in land cover, vegetation dynamics, and environmental conditions.

Machine learning models analyze multispectral imagery, extract land cover classifications, and detect land-use changes, enabling policymakers and conservationists to assess ecosystem health, identify deforestation hotspots, and prioritize conservation areas.

Water Resource Management:

A.I.-driven hydrological models simulate water flows, predict water availability, and optimize water allocation strategies in watersheds and river basins.

By integrating rainfall data, streamflow measurements, and climate projections, A.I. algorithms optimize reservoir operations, manage drought risks, and enhance water supply reliability for agricultural, industrial, and municipal purposes.

Forest Conservation and Management:

A.I. tools analyze LiDAR data, forest inventories, and canopy cover assessments to monitor forest ecosystems, quantify carbon stocks, and assess deforestation rates.

Machine learning algorithms detect illegal logging activities, map forest disturbances, and prioritize areas for reforestation and habitat restoration, contributing to the preservation of biodiversity and the mitigation of climate change impacts.

Fisheries Monitoring and Marine Conservation:

A.I.-enabled fisheries models analyze fishery data, vessel tracking information, and marine environmental variables to assess fish stocks, prevent overfishing, and promote sustainable fisheries management.

By predicting fish migration patterns, identifying fishing hotspots, and monitoring illegal fishing activities, A.I. algorithms support marine protected area designations, ecosystem-based management approaches, and the conservation of marine biodiversity.

Soil Health Assessment and Agricultural Sustainability:

A.I.-driven soil health models evaluate soil properties, nutrient levels, and erosion risks to optimize agricultural practices and promote soil conservation.

Machine learning algorithms analyze soil data, weather patterns, and crop yields to recommend precision agriculture techniques, minimize fertilizer usage, and enhance soil fertility and resilience to climate change.

Wildlife Conservation and Habitat Protection:

A.I.-powered camera traps, acoustic sensors, and wildlife tracking devices monitor animal movements, track species populations, and assess habitat connectivity.

By analyzing wildlife data, habitat suitability models, and ecological niches, A.I. algorithms inform wildlife corridors design, mitigate human-wildlife conflicts, and enhance habitat protection efforts for endangered species and biodiversity conservation.

Predictive Analytics for Climate Change and Ecosystem Preservation

In the face of escalating environmental challenges and the urgent need for proactive conservation measures, Artificial Intelligence (A.I.) emerges as a powerful tool for predicting climate change impacts and preserving fragile ecosystems. This chapter delves into the transformative role of predictive analytics in leveraging A.I. to forecast climate change trends, assess ecosystem vulnerabilities, and inform adaptive management strategies for environmental preservation.

Climate Modeling and Forecasting:

A.I.-driven climate models assimilate meteorological data, greenhouse gas emissions scenarios, and oceanic parameters to predict future climate conditions and anticipate climate change impacts.

Machine learning algorithms analyze historical climate data, atmospheric circulation patterns, and climate feedback mechanisms to forecast changes in temperature, precipitation, and extreme weather events with greater accuracy and precision.

Ecosystem Vulnerability Assessment:

A.I. tools assess ecosystem vulnerability to climate change by integrating species distribution models, habitat suitability assessments, and bioclimatic variables.

By analyzing ecological data, landscape characteristics, and climate projections, A.I. algorithms identify vulnerable ecosystems, predict shifts in species distributions, and evaluate habitat suitability under changing climatic conditions.

Biodiversity Hotspot Identification:

A.I.-powered species distribution models identify biodiversity hotspots, endemic species ranges, and areas of high conservation priority based on environmental suitability and species richness.

Machine learning algorithms analyze species occurrence records, environmental variables, and habitat characteristics to prioritize conservation efforts, designate protected areas, and safeguard critical habitats for biodiversity conservation.

Natural Disaster Prediction and Risk Assessment:

A.I. techniques such as neural networks and ensemble models predict natural disasters, including hurricanes, floods, and wildfires, by analyzing meteorological data, topographical features, and historical disaster records.

By integrating satellite imagery, climate simulations, and real-time sensor data, A.I.

algorithms forecast disaster probabilities, assess community vulnerability, and inform disaster preparedness and response efforts.

Ecosystem Service Valuation:

A.I.-driven ecosystem service models quantify the economic value of ecosystem services, including carbon sequestration, water purification, and pollination, to inform decision-making and promote sustainable land management practices.

Machine learning algorithms analyze ecosystem data, economic indicators, and societal preferences to assess the benefits of ecosystem services, prioritize conservation investments, and incentivize ecosystem stewardship.

Adaptive Management and Conservation Planning:

A.I.-enabled adaptive management frameworks integrate predictive analytics, scenario planning, and decision support systems to optimize conservation strategies and mitigate the impacts of climate change on ecosystems.

By simulating management scenarios, assessing trade-offs, and evaluating policy interventions, A.I. algorithms enable stakeholders to develop robust conservation plans, foster resilience, and adapt to changing environmental conditions.

Solutions for Sustainable Development and Conservation Efforts

In the pursuit of sustainable development and the preservation of our planet's precious resources, Artificial Intelligence (A.I.) emerges as a transformative force, offering innovative solutions to address environmental challenges and promote conservation efforts. This chapter explores the diverse applications of A.I. in advancing sustainable development goals and fostering conservation initiatives worldwide.

Smart Resource Management:

A.I.-powered optimization algorithms analyze resource consumption patterns, energy usage data, and waste generation metrics to optimize resource allocation and minimize environmental impact.

85

Machine learning models predict energy demand, optimize transportation routes, and streamline resource utilization across industries, promoting efficiency and reducing carbon emissions.

Precision Agriculture:

A.I.-driven agricultural technologies integrate satellite imagery, soil sensors, and weather forecasts to optimize crop management practices and enhance agricultural productivity.

By providing real-time insights into soil moisture levels, nutrient deficiencies, and pest outbreaks, A.I. algorithms enable farmers to make informed decisions, reduce chemical inputs, and increase crop yields sustainably.

Urban Planning and Infrastructure Development:

A.I. tools analyze urban growth patterns, demographic trends, and transportation data to inform urban planning decisions and optimize infrastructure development.

Machine learning algorithms optimize public transportation systems, design energy-efficient buildings, and mitigate urban sprawl, fostering sustainable urban development and reducing environmental degradation.

Water Conservation and Management:

A.I.-enabled water management systems monitor water quality, detect leaks, and optimize water distribution networks to ensure efficient water use and conservation.

By analyzing hydrological data, weather patterns, and demand forecasts, A.I. algorithms optimize water allocation, prioritize water conservation efforts, and mitigate the impacts of water scarcity on ecosystems and communities.

Wildlife Conservation and Anti-Poaching Efforts:

A.I.-driven surveillance systems monitor wildlife habitats, track endangered species, and detect illegal poaching activities in protected areas.

By analyzing camera trap images, acoustic data, and geospatial information, A.I. algorithms identify poaching hotspots, deploy anti-poaching patrols, and protect vulnerable wildlife populations from illegal exploitation.

Marine Conservation and Sustainable Fisheries Management:

A.I.-powered fisheries models assess fish stocks, predict fishing yields, and inform sustainable fisheries management strategies to prevent overfishing and preserve marine ecosystems.

Machine learning algorithms analyze fishing vessel movements, track fishing activities, and enforce fishing regulations, promoting responsible fishing practices and safeguarding marine biodiversity.

Community Engagement and Environmental Education:

A.I.-driven communication platforms engage communities, raise awareness, and empower individuals to participate in conservation efforts and adopt sustainable lifestyles.

By leveraging social media analytics, online forums, and educational resources, A.I. initiatives inspire collective action, foster environmental stewardship, and promote a culture of sustainability.

CHAPTER 6

CHAPTER: A.I. IN LAW ENFORCEMENT AND NATIONAL SECURITY

In the realm of law enforcement and national security, the integration of Artificial Intelligence (A.I.) technologies offers transformative capabilities to enhance threat detection, crime prevention, and public safety. This chapter explores the diverse applications of A.I. in bolstering law enforcement efforts and safeguarding national security interests.

Predictive Policing and Crime Prevention:

A.I.-powered predictive analytics analyze historical crime data, social media feeds, and demographic information to forecast crime hotspots and allocate resources efficiently.

Machine learning algorithms identify patterns of criminal activity, predict crime trends, and optimize patrol routes, enabling law enforcement agencies to deter criminal behavior and prevent crimes before they occur.

Facial Recognition and Biometric Identification:

A.I.-driven facial recognition systems analyze surveillance footage, identify suspects, and match facial images against criminal databases to enhance investigative capabilities.

Deep learning algorithms extract facial features, perform facial comparisons, and facilitate rapid identification of persons of interest, aiding law enforcement agencies in apprehending suspects and solving crimes.

Cybersecurity and Threat Intelligence:

A.I.-enabled cybersecurity platforms analyze network traffic, detect anomalous behavior, and identify potential cyber threats in real-time.

Machine learning algorithms monitor system logs, analyze malware signatures, and predict cyber attack patterns, enhancing cyber defense capabilities and

91

protecting critical infrastructure from cyber threats and data breaches.

Counterterrorism and Intelligence Analysis:

A.I. tools analyze open-source intelligence, intercepts, and communication networks to identify terrorist threats, detect radicalization trends, and disrupt terrorist activities.

Natural language processing algorithms extract insights from unstructured data, analyze communication patterns, and identify potential threats, enabling intelligence agencies to anticipate terrorist plots and prevent attacks.

Surveillance and Monitoring:

A.I.-driven surveillance systems process video feeds, monitor public spaces, and detect suspicious activities to enhance situational awareness and public safety.

Computer vision algorithms track objects, recognize behavioral patterns, and alert authorities to potential security threats, enabling rapid response and intervention in emergency situations.

Border Security and Immigration Control:

A.I.-powered border control systems analyze biometric data, scan travel documents, and perform identity verification to enhance border security and immigration control measures.

Machine learning algorithms detect fraudulent documents, identify impostors, and screen travelers against watchlists, strengthening border protection efforts and preventing illegal immigration and human trafficking.

Disaster Response and Emergency Management:

A.I.-enabled disaster response systems analyze satellite imagery, social media feeds, and sensor data to assess disaster impacts, coordinate rescue operations, and allocate resources effectively.

Machine learning algorithms predict disaster scenarios, model evacuation routes, and optimize emergency response plans, enhancing the resilience of communities and minimizing loss of life and property during natural disasters and emergencies.

Surveillance and Crime Prediction Using A.I.

In the realm of law enforcement, the integration of Artificial Intelligence (A.I.) technologies has revolutionized surveillance methods and crime prediction capabilities, empowering authorities to proactively address criminal activities and enhance public safety. This chapter explores the multifaceted applications of A.I. in surveillance and crime prediction, shedding light on its potential to mitigate crime rates and bolster security measures.

Predictive Policing Strategies:

A.I.-powered predictive policing algorithms analyze historical crime data, demographic trends, and socio-economic indicators to identify high-risk areas and predict potential crime hotspots.

Machine learning models utilize predictive analytics to forecast crime patterns, allocate resources effectively, and deploy law enforcement personnel to deter criminal activities and prevent incidents before they occur.

Behavioral Analytics and Anomaly Detection:

A.I.-driven surveillance systems monitor public spaces, analyze behavioral patterns, and detect anomalous activities indicative of criminal behavior.

Computer vision algorithms track movements, recognize suspicious behaviors, and alert authorities to potential security threats, enabling timely intervention and proactive crime prevention measures.

Facial Recognition Technology:

A.I.-enabled facial recognition systems scan crowds, analyze surveillance footage, and identify individuals of interest by matching facial features against criminal databases.

Deep learning algorithms enhance facial recognition accuracy, facilitate suspect identification, and assist law enforcement agencies in apprehending suspects and solving crimes more efficiently.

Real-Time Data Analysis and Response:

A.I.-driven surveillance platforms process real-time data streams, monitor social media feeds, and analyze digital communications to detect emerging threats and criminal activities.

Natural language processing algorithms sift through vast amounts of unstructured data, extract relevant information, and provide actionable insights to law enforcement agencies for immediate response and intervention.

Crime Trend Analysis and Resource Allocation:

A.I.-powered crime analytics tools evaluate crime trends, patterns, and correlations to inform resource allocation decisions and strategic planning for law enforcement agencies.

Machine learning algorithms identify crime clusters, assess resource demands, and optimize patrol routes, enabling law enforcement personnel to deploy resources more effectively and target crime-prone areas proactively.

Community Policing and Trust-Building Initiatives:

A.I.-enabled community policing programs leverage data-driven insights and community engagement strategies to build trust, foster collaboration, and strengthen relationships between law enforcement agencies and local communities.

A.I.-Driven Cybersecurity Measures

In an era marked by pervasive cyber threats and evolving attack vectors, Artificial Intelligence (A.I.) emerges as a critical ally in fortifying cybersecurity defenses, detecting advanced threats, and safeguarding digital assets. This chapter explores the pivotal role of A.I. in driving innovative cybersecurity measures to mitigate risks, enhance threat intelligence, and protect organizations from cyber attacks.

Threat Detection and Behavioral Analysis:

A.I.-powered cybersecurity solutions employ machine learning algorithms to analyze network traffic, user behaviors, and system activities for anomalous patterns indicative of cyber threats.

Behavioral analytics algorithms identify deviations from normal behavior, detect suspicious activities, and prioritize alerts for security analysts to investigate potential threats more efficiently.

Predictive Threat Intelligence:

A.I.-driven threat intelligence platforms collect, analyze, and correlate vast amounts of threat data from various sources to predict emerging cyber threats and vulnerabilities.

Machine learning models leverage historical attack patterns, malware signatures, and threat indicators to anticipate cyber attacks, provide early warnings, and proactively mitigate security risks.

Malware Detection and Analysis:

A.I.-enabled malware detection tools utilize pattern recognition algorithms and heuristic analysis techniques to identify and classify malicious software in real-time.

Deep learning algorithms analyze file attributes, code behavior, and network communications to detect previously unknown malware variants and prevent zero-day attacks before they can inflict damage.

Adaptive Authentication and Access Control:

A.I.-driven authentication systems employ risk-based authentication models and adaptive access controls to dynamically adjust security measures based on user behavior and contextual factors.

Machine learning algorithms assess user risk profiles, device characteristics, and geolocation data to authenticate users securely, detect suspicious login attempts, and prevent unauthorized access to sensitive resources.

Security Orchestration and Automated Response:

A.I.-powered security orchestration platforms integrate disparate security tools, automate incident response workflows, and orchestrate coordinated responses to cyber threats.

Workflow automation algorithms streamline incident triage, prioritize response actions, and facilitate collaboration among security teams, enabling rapid containment and mitigation of security incidents.

Vulnerability Management and Patch Prioritization:

A.I.-driven vulnerability management solutions analyze vulnerability data, threat intelligence feeds, and system configurations to prioritize patching and remediation efforts effectively.

Machine learning algorithms assess the severity of vulnerabilities, evaluate exploitability factors, and recommend patch deployment strategies based on the potential impact to critical assets and infrastructure.

Continuous Threat Hunting and Adversary Simulation:

A.I.-powered threat hunting platforms conduct continuous monitoring, threat hunting exercises, and red teaming simulations to proactively identify hidden threats and emulate real-world attack scenarios.

Threat hunting algorithms analyze historical incident data, conduct pattern recognition, and perform threat actor profiling to uncover sophisticated threats and strengthen cyber resilience over time.

Privacy Concerns and Legal Implications of A.I. in Security

As Artificial Intelligence (A.I.) becomes increasingly integrated into security systems and practices, it brings forth a host of privacy concerns and legal implications that must be carefully addressed. This chapter delves into the intricate balance between leveraging A.I. for security purposes while safeguarding individual privacy rights and complying with legal frameworks.

Data Privacy and Protection:

A.I.-driven security systems often rely on vast amounts of personal and sensitive data to detect threats and identify anomalies. However, the collection, storage, and processing of such data raise significant privacy concerns.

Organizations must adhere to stringent data protection regulations, such as the General Data Protection Regulation (GDPR) in the European Union and the California Consumer Privacy Act (CCPA) in the United States, to ensure the lawful and ethical handling of personal information.

Algorithmic Bias and Discrimination:

A.I. algorithms used in security applications may inadvertently perpetuate biases and discrimination, leading to unjust outcomes and infringements on individuals' rights.

It is essential to mitigate algorithmic bias by ensuring diverse and representative training datasets, transparent model development processes, and ongoing monitoring for bias and fairness.

Surveillance and Civil Liberties:

The deployment of A.I.-powered surveillance systems raises concerns about mass surveillance, government overreach, and erosion of civil liberties.

Legal frameworks and regulatory mechanisms must strike a balance between the need for public safety and the protection of individual privacy rights, ensuring that surveillance measures are proportionate, transparent, and subject to oversight.

Accountability and Transparency:

Organizations deploying A.I. in security must ensure transparency and accountability in their operations, including the use of algorithms, data handling practices, and decision-making processes.

Transparent communication with stakeholders, clear articulation of privacy policies, and mechanisms for redress and accountability are essential to build trust and maintain legitimacy in A.I.-driven security initiatives.

Legal Compliance and Regulatory Frameworks:

A.I. in security must adhere to a complex web of legal and regulatory frameworks, including privacy laws, data protection regulations, and industry standards.

Compliance with legal requirements necessitates robust data governance practices, regular risk assessments, and comprehensive privacy impact assessments to identify and mitigate potential risks to privacy and data protection.

International Collaboration and Standards:

Given the global nature of cybersecurity threats and A.I. technologies, international collaboration and harmonization of standards are crucial to address privacy concerns and ensure consistent enforcement of legal requirements.

Multilateral agreements, information-sharing mechanisms, and interoperable standards can facilitate cross-border cooperation and strengthen collective efforts to uphold privacy rights in the digital age.

CHAPTER 7

CONCLUSION

In "A.I. to the Rescue: How Artificial Intelligence Can Help Humans in Tough Situations and Make Better Decisions," we have embarked on a journey through the transformative potential of artificial intelligence (AI) in assisting humanity in various domains. From crisis response and emergency situations to healthcare, decision-making processes, safety, security, environmental conservation, and beyond, AI has emerged as a powerful tool to augment human capabilities and enhance outcomes.

Throughout our exploration, we have witnessed the remarkable ways in which AI-powered technologies are revolutionizing the landscape of problem-solving and decision-making. In crisis response, AI algorithms analyze vast datasets to predict disasters, coordinate rescue efforts, and minimize human casualties. In healthcare, AI assists in early disease detection, personalized treatment recommendations, and improving patient outcomes.

Moreover, AI has become an indispensable ally in enhancing safety and security measures, from surveillance and threat detection systems to cybersecurity and fraud prevention. Through advanced algorithms and real-time analytics, AI helps identify potential risks and vulnerabilities, enabling proactive intervention and mitigation strategies.

However, amidst the promises and potentials of AI, we must also acknowledge and address the ethical, privacy, and societal implications that accompany its widespread adoption. As we deploy AI technologies, we must prioritize transparency, accountability, fairness, and the protection of individual privacy rights.

Furthermore, collaboration and interdisciplinary dialogue are essential as we navigate the evolving landscape of AI ethics, regulation, and governance. By fostering partnerships between policymakers, technologists, ethicists, and civil society, we can ensure that AI development and deployment align with ethical principles and societal values.

In closing, "A.I. to the Rescue" serves as a testament to the symbiotic relationship between humans and artificial intelligence. By harnessing the potential of AI to augment human capabilities, we can address complex challenges, make informed decisions, and create a brighter, more resilient future for humanity. As we continue to innovate and explore the frontiers of AI technology, let us remain steadfast in our commitment to leveraging AI for the greater good and advancing the well-being of individuals and communities worldwide.

Recap of Key Points Discussed in "A.I. to the Rescue: How Artificial Intelligence Can Help Humans in Tough Situations and Make Better Decisions":

Introduction to AI's Potential: The book commenced with an exploration of the transformative potential of artificial intelligence (AI) in assisting humans across various domains, from crisis response to decision-making processes.

AI in Crisis Response: Through case studies and examples, we delved into how AI aids in predicting disasters, coordinating rescue efforts, and minimizing casualties during emergencies and natural disasters.

Healthcare and AI: The book elucidated how AI is revolutionizing healthcare, from early disease detection to personalized treatment recommendations, thereby improving patient outcomes and revolutionizing healthcare delivery.

AI in Decision-Making Processes: We examined how AI algorithms assist in complex decision-making scenarios, providing insights and recommendations to optimize outcomes across diverse industries.

Enhancing Safety and Security with AI: The book highlighted AI's role in enhancing safety and security measures through surveillance, threat detection, cybersecurity, and fraud prevention, thus safeguarding individuals, organizations, and critical infrastructure.

Environmental Conservation and Sustainability:

AI's contribution to environmental conservation and sustainability was explored, emphasizing its role in monitoring, managing resources, and mitigating the impacts of climate change.

Maintaining Ethical Boundaries:

Throughout the discussion, ethical considerations surrounding AI deployment were emphasized, emphasizing the importance of transparency, accountability, fairness, and privacy protection.

Collaboration and Governance:

The book underscored the importance of collaborative governance models and industry standards to ensure responsible AI innovation, deployment, and regulation.

Conclusion:

In conclusion, the book reinforced the symbiotic relationship between humans and AI, advocating for responsible AI development and deployment to address societal challenges and advance the well-being of humanity.

In sum, "A.I. to the Rescue" offers a comprehensive exploration of how AI can assist humans in navigating tough situations, making better decisions, and shaping a more sustainable and equitable future for all.

Affirmation of AI's Potential to Assist Humans and Improve Decision-Making

In "A.I. to the Rescue: How Artificial Intelligence Can Help Humans in Tough Situations and Make Better Decisions," the resounding affirmation of AI's potential to assist humans and enhance decision-making processes echoes throughout the book. Through thorough examination and compelling examples, it becomes evident that AI stands as a formidable ally in tackling the complex challenges facing humanity.

First and foremost, AI's capacity to process vast amounts of data and identify patterns transcends human capabilities, enabling unparalleled insights and predictions. Whether in crisis response, healthcare, or environmental conservation, AI empowers

110

humans to make informed decisions based on data-driven analysis and forecasts.

Moreover, AI serves as a catalyst for innovation across industries, revolutionizing traditional approaches to problem-solving and decision-making. From optimizing resource allocation to enhancing security measures, AI-driven solutions enable organizations and individuals to navigate tough situations with agility and foresight.

Furthermore, AI's potential to augment human intelligence and creativity is boundless. By automating routine tasks and providing decision support, AI liberates humans to focus on higher-order thinking, innovation, and problem-solving, thereby unlocking new frontiers of discovery and advancement.

Indeed, the affirmation of AI's potential to assist humans extends beyond mere utility; it encompasses a vision of empowerment, collaboration, and progress. As we embrace AI as a transformative force for good, we unlock endless possibilities for addressing societal challenges, improving individual well-being, and shaping a more resilient and sustainable future for generations to come.

Call to Action for Responsible Development and Deployment of AI Technologies

As we conclude our exploration in "A.I. to the Rescue: How Artificial Intelligence Can Help Humans in Tough Situations and Make Better Decisions," it is imperative to heed the call for responsible development and deployment of AI technologies. The transformative potential of AI comes with significant ethical, societal, and regulatory considerations that demand our attention and action.

Ethical Frameworks and Guidelines: We must establish clear ethical frameworks and guidelines to govern the development and deployment of AI technologies. These frameworks should prioritize transparency, accountability, fairness, and privacy protection, ensuring that AI systems are designed and used in a manner that aligns with societal values and principles.

Collaborative Governance Models: Collaboration between governments, industry stakeholders, academia, and civil society is essential in shaping responsible AI policies and regulations. By fostering interdisciplinary dialogue and cooperation, we can address complex ethical and regulatory challenges and ensure that AI innovation serves the public interest.

Education and Awareness: Education and awareness initiatives play a crucial role in fostering a culture of responsible AI adoption. We must equip individuals, organizations, and policymakers with the knowledge and skills needed to understand the ethical implications of AI technologies and make informed decisions about their development and deployment.

Transparency and Accountability: Transparency and accountability are paramount in building trust and confidence in AI systems. Developers and organizations must be transparent about the capabilities, limitations, and potential biases of AI algorithms, while mechanisms for accountability should be established to address instances of algorithmic discrimination or misuse.

Privacy Protection and Data Governance:

As AI relies heavily on data, robust privacy protection and data governance mechanisms are essential to safeguarding individual privacy rights. Data collection, storage, and processing practices must adhere to data protection laws and ethical standards, ensuring that personal information is handled responsibly and ethically.

Continuous Evaluation and Monitoring:

AI systems should undergo continuous evaluation and monitoring to assess their impact on society, identify potential biases or risks, and mitigate unintended consequences. Regular audits and evaluations can help ensure that AI technologies remain aligned with ethical principles and societal values throughout their lifecycle.

Global Collaboration and Standards:

Given the global nature of AI

technology, international collaboration and the development of common standards are essential in promoting responsible AI development and deployment worldwide. By fostering collaboration between countries and regions, we can harmonize regulatory approaches and promote ethical best practices on a global scale.

In conclusion, the responsible development and deployment of AI technologies are not merely aspirations but imperatives for shaping a future where AI serves as a force for good. By embracing ethical principles, fostering collaboration, and prioritizing societal well-being, we can harness the full potential of AI to address pressing challenges, empower individuals and communities, and create a more equitable and sustainable world for all.